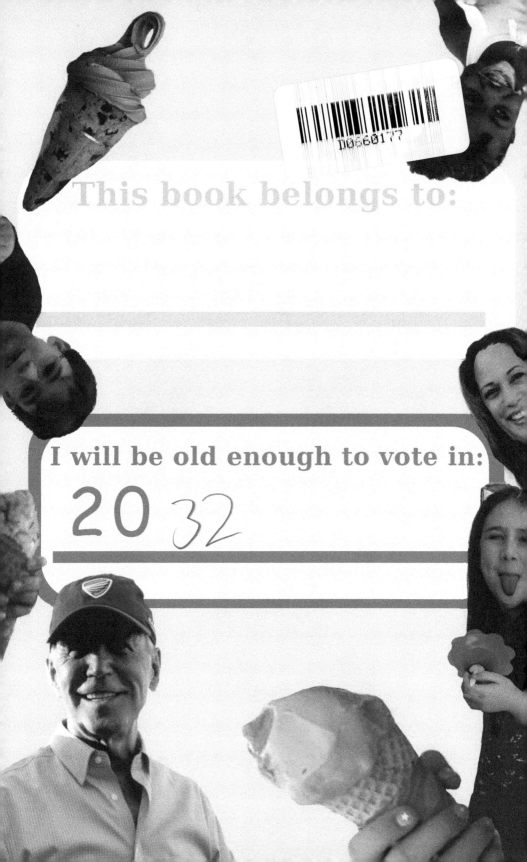

This book belongs to:

I will be old enough to vote in:

20 *32*

Joe Biden:

WHO IS AMERICA'S 46TH PRESIDENT?

R.L. MARGOLIN

J. Emmett Press ✦

For my grandmother,

who passed on the importance of voting through stories of the suffragettes in our family tree.

JemmettPress@gmail.com

ISBN 978-1-0879-1448-0

The illustrations in this book were created using digital photography and digital collage.

Joe Biden is the 46th president of the United States.

He works with Vice President Kamala Harris.

Early Life

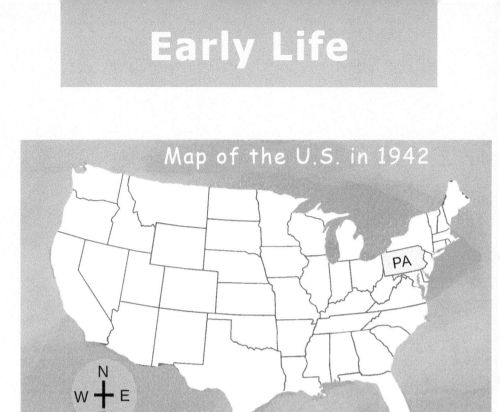

Map of the U.S. in 1942

Joseph Robinette Biden Jr. was born on November 20, 1942 in Scranton, Pennsylvania to Catherine "Jean" and Joseph Biden Sr. He was their first child and would become a big brother to Val, Frank, and Jim. The Biden family was Catholic. They went to church on Sundays and sent their children to religious schools.

3

As a boy, Joe liked a good challenge. On a dare he would do risky stunts to impress other kids. He also liked sports. Even as a little guy, he played football with kids who were bigger and older.

Joe liked to play football.

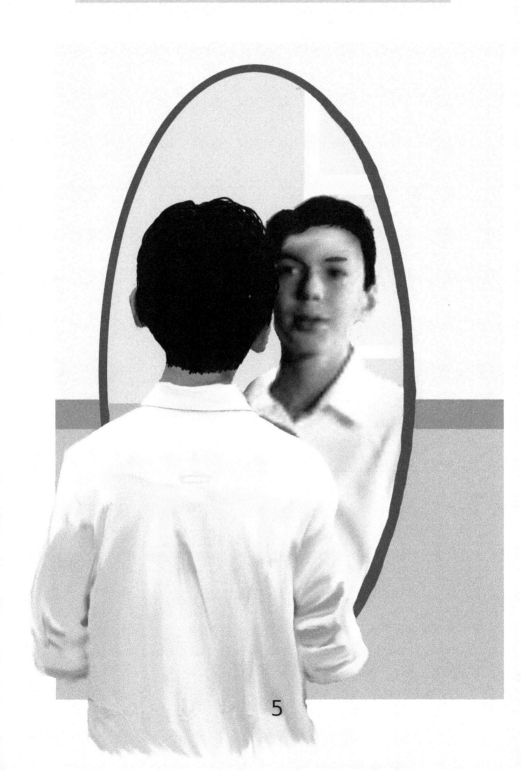

When Joe was ten years old, his dad had trouble finding work in Scranton. The Biden family moved to Delaware, where his dad found a job selling cars.

Joe had a speech problem. He wanted to speak clearly, but sometimes he would **stutter.** Some kids, and even some adults would tease him, calling him "B-b-b-b-Biden!" His mom encouraged him, "Joey nobody is better than you. You're not better than anybody else, but *nobody* is any better than you." His teacher encouraged him too, and gave him a hint, "You can beat the stutter with practice." Joe worked hard, repeating poems in front of a mirror. If he had to read out loud in class, he would practice the night before too. It helped!

Archmere Academy

Joe also worked hard to reach other
goals. He wanted to go to a great school
called Archmere Academy, but **tuition**
was a lot of money. His parents did not
have enough money to pay for the
school.

7

Joe washed many windows.

Joe made a deal with the school. He
would pay his way by working for the
school in the summer. He cleaned a lot
of windows. He painted the fence. He
worked in the garden.

Joe wanted to become a lawyer. He studied history, political science, and English at the University of Delaware. Then he studied law at the University of Syracuse.

Syracuse University College of Law

Joe had time for fun too. He took a vacation with college friends to the beach. Neilia Hunter was visiting the same beach with her college friends, and she had a chat with Joe. In time, they fell in love and got married. They had three children, Beau, Hunter, and Naomi.

Joe and Neilia's lakeside wedding party.

Neilia had a career as a teacher. She also worked with Joe to help him reach his dream of becoming a lawyer, and then a senator. Sadly, right after Joe became a senator, his family had a bad car accident. Neilia and Naomi died, Beau and Hunter were hurt and spent a long time in the hospital. It was a hard time for the Bidens.

Joe had a big job to do as a senator for Delaware, but he also had two young boys at home who needed a lot of love. Joe's sister Val moved in to help, and Joe tried to do it all. Every day, he would eat breakfast with Hunter and Beau. Then Joe took a train to work as a senator in Washington D.C., but he made sure he was home each night in time to tuck them into bed.

Joe became a leader in the Senate. He worked with other senators to write laws to keep Americans safe from crime and to protect important freedoms called **civil liberties**. He found a way to work things out, even when he strongly disagreed with another senator on a law.

Joe also led the Senate through some important decisions about who should become a judge on the **U.S. Supreme Court**. The U.S. Supreme Court has a lot of power over the country's laws, so it is very important that the judges on that court will make decisions that are fair to all Americans. When the Court needs a new judge, the president picks someone for the job. If the senators agree with the president, the new judge gets the job. If the senators don't agree, the president chooses another person.

While Joe was a senator, his brother Frank introduced him to Jill Jacobs. Jill had a career as a teacher, and she liked to run in races.

Joe and Jill fell in love. Beau and Hunter liked her too. "When are we going to get married?" they asked Joe. The boys got their wish. Joe and Jill got married, and together they had a daughter named Ashley.

Vice President

Joe thought about becoming president of the U.S. He started to run for president in 1988, but he didn't win. Joe went back to work in the Senate. In 2008 he ran for president again. He didn't win that time either. Barack Obama won, but he chose Joe Biden as his vice president.

As vice president, Joe worked with President Obama.

Joe meets the troops.

As vice president, Joe worked with President Obama to try to solve problems for the American people. They ran projects to build communities, which also gave Americans good jobs. They made a plan to bring American troops working far away back home. Together with the lawmakers in Congress, they passed laws to keep people safer from guns.

16

Joe Biden did a lot of serious work as vice president, but he also had some fun. He became known for wearing cool sunglasses and eating ice cream cones.

He worked with President Obama on important jobs, but they were also good friends. Joe even joked about making friendship bracelets for them.

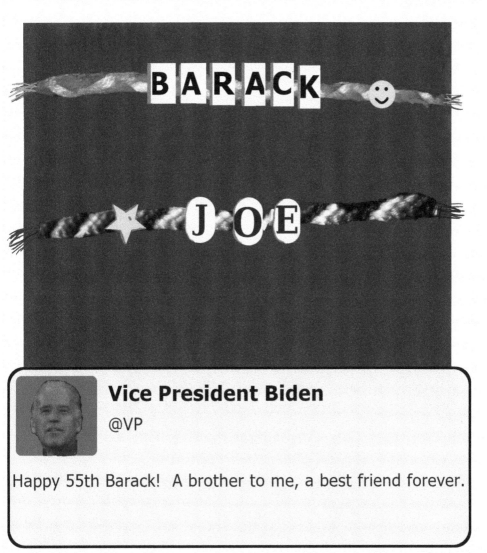

Vice President Biden
@VP

Happy 55th Barack! A brother to me, a best friend forever.

They played golf together.

They watched sports together, like basketball
and tennis. 20

Some days they even matched ties!

President

Barack Obama's last **term** as president ended in 2016. Joe could have run to be the next president, but he decided not to. He wasn't done yet though, and he decided to run for president in 2020. This time he won!

President Joe Biden and Vice President Kamala Harris are teamed up to help Americans. They have big plans. They want the U.S. to have factories to make the things Americans need, and so Americans will have good jobs.

Solar panel factory

Solar roof panels

They want to make the U.S. more friendly to the Earth. The many gas powered cars in the U.S. **pollute** the air. If Americans have electric cars, and there are trains and buses in more towns, the air will be clean and healthy. Joe has plans to build **green transportation** in the U.S.

Public bus

Train station

Child Care

Senior Care

Joe has plans to help families. Children need a safe place to learn and play while adults go to work. Some adults are not healthy enough to live alone, and need care to stay safe. Too often, families have a hard time finding daycare. Joe wants to build communities, so families can find great care close to home.

Joe and Kamala are working together to make a better future for all Americans. What can you do to help your community today? What will you do when you grow up?

Glossary

Civil liberties- freedoms from too much government control; includes the right to have your own opinions and share them with other people, to meet up with other people, to make your own decisions about religion, and many more.

Green transportation- ways to travel that do not hurt the Earth.

Pollute- to make dirty, especially when talking about making the air, water, and ground unhealthy with waste.

Senate- part of the U.S. government; senators are elected to decide what the law should be.

Stutter- a kind of speech challenge; a person who stutters may repeat sounds, or have a hard time saying some words.

Term- how long a person elected to do a job can work before it is time for another election; in the United States a president's term is four years.

Tuition- the fee for being a student at a school.

U.S. Supreme Court- highest court in the U.S.

Dear Grown-ups,

Did your child enjoy this book?
Support independent publishing by leaving an online review!

Your candid review at your favorite online bookseller will help other parents, grandparents, teachers, and librarians to decide if this book is right for their children.

Please share this book with your network on social media.

Many Thanks,
R. L. Margolin

Sources:

Background information:

Biden, Joe. *Joe Biden, Promises To Keep.* Random House, Inc., 2007.

Wilser, Jeff. *The Book of Joe: The Life, Wit, and (Sometimes Accidental) Wisdom of Joe Biden.* Three Rivers Press, 2017.

www.joebiden.com

Photo Credits: The illustrations in this book were created using digital photographs as a part of a digital collage. Some photos are authentic, like the picture of a building at Syracuse University. Other photos are an imaginative depiction, like the picture of a young Joe Biden practicing speaking in front of a mirror. This background scene was drawn with digital pen, while depiction of Joe is actually two photos of different boys who resemble a ten year old Joe Biden. Many thanks to the open source Creative Commons community for sharing the digital photographs used to illustrate this book!

Licensing Information: Each photo offers specific licenses and attribution requirements for use. For links to licensing information, please use the citations to locate the photos on on www.creativecommons.org.

Image Alteration: All original images cited here have been altered for use in this publication Original images may have been cropped, stretched, or merged with original digital art.

Image Sources

Page 1 "Joe Biden at McKinley Elementary School" by Phil Roeder
 "Vice President Joe Biden has breakfast with the troops [Image 1 of 11]" by DVIDSHUB
Page 2 "Kamala Harris" by Gage Skidmore
Page 3   "Map of the United States (Generic)" by DonkeyHotey
Page 4 "Colts Football" by pocketwiley
Page 5 "Reading is fun" by photogramma1
 "YBQC chorus-4510" by Barbershop Harmony Society
Page 7 "Archmere" by jimmywayne
Page 8 "Durkee Mansion windows (4)" by MaryLouiseEklund
Page 9 "Syracuse University" by runJMrun
Page 10 "File:20090120 Jill and Joe Biden at Homestates Ball.JPG" by TonyTheTiger
"outdoor wedding" by JeniLegs

Page 24 "Helen Listening to Sophia Play the Harp" by Pictures by Ann
"Boca West Foundation - Boys and Girls Club - Old Navy - 2017" by CLender
"Ambassador Kids Club at the Grand Velas Riveria Maya" by Grand Velas Riviera Maya
Page 25 "Kamala Harris with supporter" by Gage Skidmore
"Kamala Harris" by quinn.anya
"Joe Biden with supporter" by Gage Skidmore
"131207 - Vice President Biden visits Korea" by UNC - CFC - USFK
"Joe Biden with supporters" by Gage Skidmore i
Indian child "Children Reading Pratham Books and Akshara" by Pratham Books
"Black Girl Head Band Natural Hair" by stevendepolo

Cover Images
"Joe Biden" by Gage Skidmore
Balloons "083012_MittRomney_023" by NewsHour
Star balloon Image by Mayra F.

CPSIA information can be obtained
at www.ICGtesting.com
Printed in the USA
LVHW071614301120
672815LV00005BA/69